Mel Bay's

MUSIC ESS

CW00386501

BASIC MUSIC THEORY
FOR ALL INSTRUMENTS

by Charles Chapman

QWIKGUIDE®

1 2 3 4 5 6 7 8 9 0

Visit us on the Web at www.melbay.com — E-mail us at email@melbay.com

TABLE OF CONTENTS

FOREWORD

No matter what instrument you may play there are music essentials that bridge the gaps between styles and musical genres. Understanding these inner workings of the musical world will open up an awareness and creativity you never dreamed possible.

This brief tome covers the basic elements used in modern contemporary music. The material is divided into three sections: Theory, Harmony and Notation. They are not totally separate identities and most of the material could actually fit into any of the categories listed. By "pigeon-holing", what many consider these elusive elements, it tends to be easier to explain and understand the craft of this wonderful art form we call music.

With minimal theoretical knowledge this text should be self-explanatory, but using it in conjunction with a knowledgeable instructor will definitely help you relate it to your individual instrument.

Chapter 1
THEORY
Staff

The staff is the fundamental symbol in music notation. It is made up of five lines and four spaces on, or around, which all forms of notation are placed.

The lines and spaces provide a location for specific pitch* and duration. Symbols and terms are placed around it to tell the player how loud or soft, or how long or short a note should be played. In musical terms these are referred to as dynamics* and articulations*.

For reference purposes, any time the number of a line or space is stated it will be referred to as follows:

Lines   Spaces

5   4
4   3
3   2
2   1
1

* Pitch - A term referring to the high-low quality of a musical sound.

* Duration - How long in time a sound lasts.

* Dynamics - Words or signs indicating degrees or changes of loudness.

* Articulation - A symbol or term used to denote the manner in which a note is attacked, such as staccato, legato, or accents.

THEORY
Clefs

The clef designates fixed locations of specific pitch degrees and is always located at the very beginning of the first staff. On parts* and lead sheets*, the clefs are generally only at the beginning of the first line of each page. In classical literature, however, a clef is placed at the beginning of every line.

For general purposes the only clefs you will need to be aware of are the treble and bass clef.

Contemporary instruments that use this clef:

Treble Clef

Guitar	- This includes all types; acoustic, electric, classical.
Keyboards	- Lead sheets are generally written only in treble clef for any keyboard. This includes acoustic or electric piano, organ, synthesizer, etc.
Mandolin	
Banjo	- Four or five string.
Violin	
Trumpet	- Flugelhorn and coronet.
Saxophone	- Alto, tenor and soprano.

Contemporary instruments that use this clef:

Bass Clef

Bass Guitar	- Also bass violin.
Trombone	- Slide or valve
Baritone Sax	

Alternate Clefs

Alto Clef

Viola

Percussion Clef

Tenor Clef

Bassoon
Tenor Trombone
High range of Cello

Bass clef is the traditional way of notating percussion parts, but in contempory music the percussion clef is now used most of the time.

*Lead Sheet - A basic melodic line in concert key usually with chord changes.
Parts - A melodic line which is transposed from concert key for the individual instrument.*

THEORY
Note Durations With Corresponding Rest Values

Note values have sustained sound while rest values have the equivalent amount of silence

A dot added to the right of the note adds one half of the note's value to the note, and the same applies to the rests.

Dotted whole note = 6 beats
Dotted half note = 3 beats
Dotted quarter note = 1 1/2 beats
Dotted eighth note = 3/4 of a beat

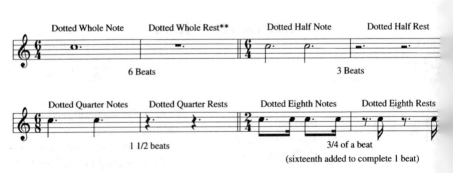

* *If you want to make an entire measure blank, use a whole rest regardless of the time signature. Do not, for instance, use a half rest in 2/4.*
** *Rarely used. For six beats of rest, it's better to use a combination of smaller rest*

THEORY
Time Signatures

The time signature appears directly after the clef and the key signature. The time signature consists of two numbers vertically aligned; it is placed only at the beginning of the piece or when the time changes. When the time signature changes, there is no need to use a new clef unless that is changing also. The upper number instructs how may beats in each measure and the lower indicates the chosen unit of measurement (half note, quarter note, etc.).

Listed below are some time signatures seen in contemporary music:

The most common time signature used is 4/4, and may also be referred to as common time. A "℃" may be used in place of 4/4.

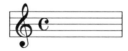

Do not confuse common time with cut time. Cut time, or alla breve*, refers to cutting the time value in half. It is equivalent to 2/2. This is the common time sign with a line through the middle.

Alla breve - (AH-la BRAY-vay) A tempo mark indicated by the sign ¢, for quick double time, with the half note rather than the quarter note as the beat. In other words, 2/2 instead of 4/4.

THEORY
Key Signatures

♯ Sharp = This symbol raises the note one half step

♭ Flat = This symbol lowers the note one half step

♮ Natural = This symbols cancels either a sharp or a flat

The key signature instructs what notes must be altered throughout the piece. It affects all octaves until a new key signature occurs. The key signature is placed directly after the clef and before the time signature.

Listed below are the most common major key signatures:

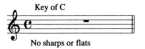

Key of C
No sharps or flats

Key of G
(F♯)

Key of D
(F♯, C♯)

Key of A
(F♯, C♯, G♯)

Key of E
(F♯, C♯, G♯, D♯)

Key of B
F♯, C♯, G♯, D♯, A♯

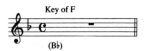

Key of F
(B♭)

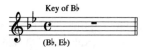

Key of B♭
(B♭, E♭)

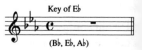

Key of E♭
(B♭, E♭, A♭)

Key of A♭
(B♭, E♭, A♭, D♭)

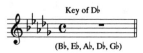

Key of D♭
(B♭, E♭, A♭, D♭, G♭)

Key of G♭
B♭, E♭, A♭, D♭, G♭, C♭

* These keys are what are commonly seen in most written music. Other key signatures such as F♯, C♯ and C♭ do exist – but are not the norm.

THEORY
Dynamics

Dynamics and articulations are often omitted in lead sheets or by amateur musicians. The general rule is that when there are no dynamics or articulations indicated, the music is performed as the style dictates. I personally feel this sometimes leaves too much for the individual musician to interpret.

The following is a list of dynamics that the contemporary musician must know and be able to use correctly. Tradition dictates that the Italian terms for dynamics always be indicated.

Term	Abbreviation	Translation
pianissimo	*pp*	very soft
piano	*p*	soft
mezzo-piano	*mp*	medium soft
mezzo forte	*mf*	medium loud
forte	*f*	loud
fortissimo	*ff*	very loud

Always use abbreviations, never the full name; also, lower case letters are always used rather that capitals. For single-staff instruments, dynamics should always be placed beneath the staff, directly below or slightly to the left of the first note. Once a dynamic level is indicated it is maintained until a new one appears.

THEORY
Dynamics

To indicate a gradual increase or decrease in volume, the following terms may be used:

Term	Abbreviation	Translation
crescendo	cresc.	increase in volume
diminuendo	dim.	decrease in volume
decrescendo	decresc.	decrease in volume

Diminuendo and decrescendo mean the same and are interchangeable. I personally prefer to use decrescendo.

To indicate a gradual increase or decrease in volume for a short duration, "wedges" or "hairpins" are used instead of verbal terms.

THEORY
Repeats

The repeat sign consists of a double bar and two dots as follows:

The general rule governing repeat signs is that you repeat back to the nearest repeat sign facing the opposite direction, if there are none, return to the beginning of the piece.

Both of the above examples notate the exact same music. I personally use repeat signs on both ends, as I find it the best way to avoid confusion.

The single measure repeat sign is another notational shortcut. This symbol instructs the performer to repeat the previous measure once.

If more than one measure is to be repeated indicate above the measure the number of previous measures that are to be repeated.

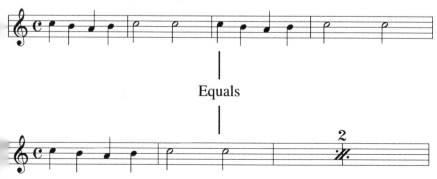

Equals

THEORY
Repeats & Tempo Indications

First and Second Endings are a musical shortcut that can save a great deal of writing and paper. It indicates the first time you play to the repeat sign, then return to the beginning of the section that is to be repeated. The second time you skip the first ending and play the second ending.

A 1st or 2nd ending does not necessarily have to be only one measure long. Endings can be any length, within reason.

If an exact tempo is critical to a piece of music, a metronome* marking should be used.

Rock Ballad   ♩ =100   This indicates that the tempo is equal to one hundred quarter notes per minute.

While the usual notation indicates how many times a quater note beats per minute, for fast tempos or unusual time signatures, other note values can be used.

𝅗𝅥 =100   This indicates that there are one hundred half notes per minute

𝅗𝅥. = 60   This indicates that there are sixty dotted half notes per minute.

*Metronome - An apparatus that sounds regular beats at adjustable speeds.

12

THEORY
Articulations

The three most common articulations are staccato (.), legato (—), and accent (>)

Staccato indicates that the note should be played short. A good way to visualize this is to think of the note as being "hot" and to get off it as quickly as possible. It is indicated by a dot above the staff and generally applied to notes with a duration of one beat or less.

Legato means to play the note as smoothly as possible, usually with a soft dull attack. The symbol for legato is a dash over the note. The general rule is, if there are no articulations present, the notes are assumed to be played legato.

An accent indicates that the note should receive an emphasized attack. The duration of the note is not altered and the accent is drawn as a small wedge over the note affected.

Fermata and Caesura

A fermata* is commonly referred to as a "hold" or "birdseye." It instructs the player to hold a note or rest until cued to continue. The caesura* commonly referred to as "railroad tracks" or a "cut" sign, indicates that player should immediately stop playing and not continue until cued.

Fermata   Caesura

Often the fermata is used in conjunction with a caesura.

These symbols are generally only used in studio or orchestra context where a conductor is present. The exception is solo performances where the performer may use his or her discretion.

THEORY
Roadmaps

Being able to read a roadmap is advantageous when traveling in an unfamiliar area. The same is true for musicians reading a piece of music for the first time. Many times charts and lead sheets often utilize short cuts such as repeats, endings, etc. Being able to correctly interppret these markings can mean the difference between playing a piece of music correctly and going frantic trying to figure out where you should be. The following shortcuts are what I consider to be the most common.

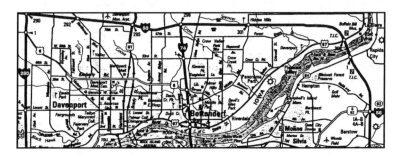

D. 𝄋 or D.S. = Play from sign (𝄋)

D.C. = Play from the beginning

D. 𝄋 (S.R.) or D.S. (S.R.) = Play from the sign without repeats

D. 𝄋 (C.R.) or D.S. (C.R.) = Play from the sign with repeats

D.C. (S.R.) = Play from the beginning without repeats

D.C. (C.R.) = Play from the beginning with repeats

*Unwritten Rule: Play only 2nd endings after D.𝄋 or D.C. if not notated otherwise.

Fine = The End

D.C. al Fine = Go to the beginning and stop at Fine.

Segue = Continue on without stopping

V.S. = Turn page

Abbreviation	Derivation
D.C.	Da Capo
D.𝄋 or D.S.	Dal Segno
S.R.	Senza Repeats
C.R.	Con Repeats
V.S.	Volti Subito

Chapter 2
HARMONY
Harmonic Food-Chain

Harmony has a long lineage that has passed the test of time. To understand the way harmony works we must start from the bottom and work our way up—or as my students call it: "The Harmonic Food Chain."

First and foremost, we must know and understand our major key signatures and their respective tonal degrees (see pages 16 & 17). The next step is triadic harmony (pages 18), then seventh chords (page 19) and finally chord extensions (23 & 24).

The true hierarchy of the food chain is the chord or harmonic extensions. These tones are what some refer to as jazz chords. This elite group of chords is generally misunderstood, misused and flaunted shamelessly by amateurs and professionals alike.

When learning the inner workings of harmony the most important aspect is to follow the natural rules of the food chain and make sure you thoroughly understand and can function with each step before going on.

HARMONY
Scale Degrees

There are seven degrees or notes in all major scales with the first one being referred to as the root. All other major scale degrees are numbered in numerical order.

Key of C

Sharp Keys

HARMONY
Scale Degrees

Flat Keys

HARMONY
Chord Formulas For Triads

MAJOR	MINOR	DIMINISHED	AUGMENTED
R35	R♭35	R♭3♭5	R3♯5

Key of C

MAJOR	MINOR	DIMINISHED	AUGMENTED
CEG	CE♭G	CE♭G♭	CEG♯

Sharp Keys

KEY	MAJOR	MINOR	DIMINISHED	AUGMENTED
G	GBD	GB♭D	GB♭D♭	GBD♯
D	DF♯A	DFA	DFA♭	DF♯A♯
A	AC♯E	ACE	ACE♭	AC♯E♯
E	EG♯B	EGB	EGB♭	EG♯B♯
B	BD♯F♯	BDF♯	BDF	BD♯F×*

(× = ♯♯)

Flat Keys

KEY	MAJOR	MINOR	DIMINISHED	AUGMENTED
F	FAC	FA♭C	FA♭C♭	FAC♯
B♭	B♭DF	B♭D♭F	B♭D♭F♭	B♭DF♯
E♭	E♭GB♭	E♭G♭B♭	E♭G♭B♭♭*	E♭GB
A♭	A♭CE♭	A♭C♭E♭	A♭C♭E♭♭	A♭CE
D♭	D♭FA♭	D♭F♭A♭	D♭F♭A♭♭	D♭F♭A
G♭	G♭B♭D♭	G♭B♭♭D♭	G♭B♭♭D♭♭	G♭B♭♭D

* double-sharp raises the note two half-steps
double-flat lowers the note two half-steps

HARMONY
Chord Formulas For Commonly Used 7th Chords

DOM. 7TH	MAJ. 7TH	MIN. 7TH	MIN. 7TH Flat 5	DIM. 7TH
R35♭7	R357	R♭35♭7	R♭3♭5♭7	R♭3♭5♭♭7

Key of C

DOM. 7TH	MAJ. 7TH	MIN. 7TH	MIN. 7TH ♭5	DIM. 7TH
CEGB♭	CEGB	CE♭GB♭	CE♭G♭B♭	CE♭G♭B♭♭

Sharp Keys

KEY	DOM. 7TH	MAJ. 7TH	MIN. 7TH	MIN. 7TH ♭5	DIM. 7TH
G	GBDF	GBDF♯	GB♭DF	GB♭D♭F	GB♭D♭F♭
D	DF♯AC	DF♯AC♯	DFAC	DFA♭C	DFA♭C♭
A	AC♯EG	AC♯EG♯	ACEG	ACE♭G	ACE♭G♭
E	EG♯BD	EG♯BD♯	EGBD	EGB♭D	EGB♭D♭
B	BD♯F♯A	BD♯F♯A♯	BDF♯A	BDFA	BDFA♭

Flat Keys

KEY	DOM. 7TH	MAJ. 7TH	MIN. 7TH	MIN. 7TH ♭5	DIM. 7TH
F	FACE♭	FACE	FA♭CE♭	FA♭C♭E♭	FA♭C♭E♭♭
B♭	B♭DFA♭	B♭DFA	B♭D♭FA♭	B♭D♭F♭A♭	B♭D♭F♭A♭♭
E♭	E♭GB♭D♭	E♭GB♭D	E♭G♭B♭D♭	E♭G♭B♭♭D♭	E♭G♭B♭♭D♭♭
A♭	A♭CE♭G♭	A♭CE♭G	A♭C♭E♭G♭	A♭C♭E♭♭G♭	A♭C♭E♭♭G♭♭
D♭	D♭FA♭C♭	D♭FA♭C	D♭F♭A♭C♭	D♭F♭A♭♭C♭	D♭F♭A♭♭C♭♭
G♭	G♭B♭D♭F♭	G♭B♭D♭F	G♭B♭♭D♭F♭	G♭B♭♭D♭♭F♭	G♭B♭♭D♭♭F♭♭

HARMONY
Diatonic Chords

Diatonic means to build chord forms from a specific scale. For example, in the key of C major only notes from that scale could be used in constructing diatonic chords. The most common diatonic chords are constructed with four notes built up in 3rds. These chords will follow the same harmonic/numerical order no matter what key they are in. The following are the diatonic chords for the 12 basic major keys.

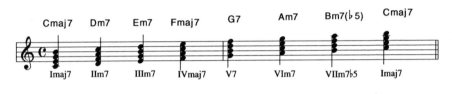

Sharp Keys

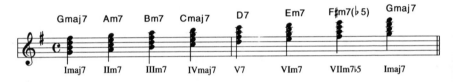

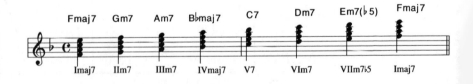

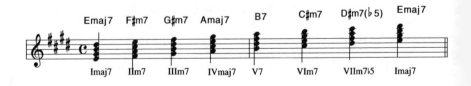

HARMONY
Diatonic Chords

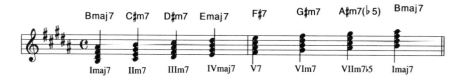

Bmaj7 C#m7 D#m7 Emaj7 F#7 G#m7 A#m7(♭5) Bmaj7

Imaj7 IIm7 IIIm7 IVmaj7 V7 VIm7 VIIm7♭5 Imaj7

Flat Keys

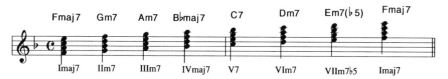

Fmaj7 Gm7 Am7 B♭maj7 C7 Dm7 Em7(♭5) Fmaj7

Imaj7 IIm7 IIIm7 IVmaj7 V7 VIm7 VIIm7♭5 Imaj7

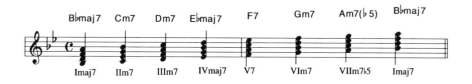

B♭maj7 Cm7 Dm7 E♭maj7 F7 Gm7 Am7(♭5) B♭maj7

Imaj7 IIm7 IIIm7 IVmaj7 V7 VIm7 VIIm7♭5 Imaj7

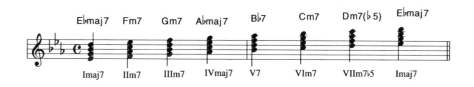

E♭maj7 Fm7 Gm7 A♭maj7 B♭7 Cm7 Dm7(♭5) E♭maj7

Imaj7 IIm7 IIIm7 IVmaj7 V7 VIm7 VIIm7♭5 Imaj7

D♭maj7 E♭m7 Fm7 G♭maj7 A♭7 B♭m7 Cm7(♭5) D♭maj7

Imaj7 IIm7 IIIm7 IVmaj7 V7 VIm7 VIIm7♭5 Imaj7

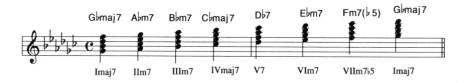

G♭maj7 A♭m7 B♭m7 C♭maj7 D♭7 E♭m7 Fm7(♭5) G♭maj7

Imaj7 IIm7 IIIm7 IVmaj7 V7 VIm7 VIIm7♭5 Imaj7

HARMONY
IIm7 V7 Imaj7 Progression

One of the most predominant chord progressions in any style of music is the IIm7 V7 Imaj7 progression. This means that you play the diatonic chords constructed from the 2nd, 5th and 1st degrees of the major scale.

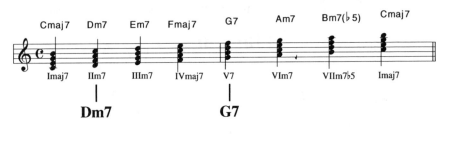

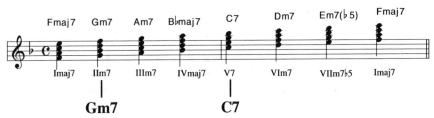

IIm7- V7 - Imaj7 Progressions In All Major keys

Key	IIm	V7	Imaj7		Key	IIm	V7	Imaj7
C =	Dm7	G7	Cma7					
G =	Am7	D7	Gmaj7		F =	Gm7	C7	Fma7
D =	Em7	A7	Dmaj7		B♭ =	Cm7	F7	B♭maj7
A =	Bm7	E7	Amaj7		E♭ =	Fm7	B♭7	E♭maj7
E =	F♯m7	B7	Emaj7		A♭ =	B♭m7	E♭7	A♭maj7
B =	C♯m7	F♯7	Bmaj7		D♭ =	E♭m7	A♭7	D♭maj7

HARMONY
Chord Extensions

Chord extensions are sometimes referred to as just tensions, and are the logical extensions of the basic chord. These are the most misunderstood, misused and over played in the harmonic food chain.

To start with you should be familiar with what I call the tension equivalents.

2=9
4=11
6=13

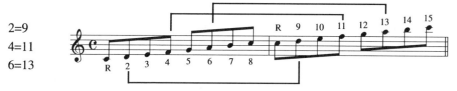

One would presume by that the difference between 2 & 9, 4 & 11, and 6 & 13 are merely an octave. The reality is this is an untruth. What makes a chord an extension is that it is based over a dominant 7th chord (unless otherwise stipulated) and the range the note falls in has nothing to do with it, even though in most cases the extension is above the octave.

C9 = R 3 5 ♭7 9 = C E G B♭ D   C11 = R 3 5 ♭7 11 = C E G B♭ F

C13 = R 3 5 ♭7 13 = C E G B♭ A   F6 = R 3 5 6 = F A C D

F13 = R 3 5 ♭7 13 = F A C E♭ D

Note that on the F6 and on the F13 that the D is the same note. If there is a ♭7 present the D will be a 13, if there is no ♭7 present the D will be a 6.

HARMONY
Chord Extensions

If a natural 7 (major 7) is desired the chord symbol must state:

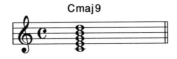

If no 7th of any kind is desired the lower case number is used or it is stipulated in some other manner:

C6 = R 3 5 6 = C E G A

C2 or C (add9) = R 3 5 2 (or add9)

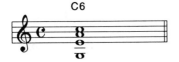

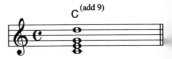

The secret to performing tensions in an expedient manner is to be aware that all the notes in the chord are not needed to be played. The root and/or the 5th can be eliminated at any time to achieve a clearer sound or ease of fingering. This is a very effective technique especially when a bass player is present.

C7 (♭9, ♯11) = R 3 5 ♭7 ♭9 ♯11 = C E G B♭ D♭ F♯

C7 (♯9 ♭13) = R 3 5 ♭7 ♯9 ♭13 = C E G B♭ D♯ A♭

Chapter 3
NOTATION

Technology is flying at warp speed as we enter the new millennium where cyber-musicians and the technology super highway are the norm. As equipment, styles and the manner in which we access information change, one aspect of music never budges—the manner musicians in general notate their musical thoughts. Whether it be in traditional notation, tablature, or any form of written musical expression it's often close to being illegible to anyone but themselves.

With the entry of computers into the arsenal of musicians' tools, many feel the need for legible and accurate notation skills has become a thing of the past. The computer, they argue, can produce professional-quality printed music with unprecedented opportunities for last minute changes. The problem is that most music software packages offer choices of parameters and placement. If you do not know the essential elements of music your written musical thoughts may become nothing more than very neat, illegible, inaccurate notation. Also, while the computer is a definite plus, and is truly the best way to now notate and store music, hand notation is still the mode most musicians initially jot down their initial musical brainstorms.

In this chapter all examples are notated with a metal roller point pen or pencil (with a lead thickness of 0.9). Also, a clear six inch ruler is helpful when beaming and for stems to insure a neat look and proper alignment.

With a few basic rules (that many never think about), your musical thoughts will now take on a fresh new life. The fact is, the more legible your music looks, the more your art-form will be taken seriously.

NOTATION
Spacial Notation

Avoid Crowding Your Work
Usually four measures to a line is the recommended amount unless you have a 3/4 or 2/4 time signature. An active measure should take up more space than an inactive one. Also try to fill up all the staffs with music and never use only part of a staff if possible.

Poor Spacing

Good Spacing and Layout

Avoid Artistic Alterations
Avoid artistic calligraphy, fancy swirls on eighth note tails, or any other "artistic" alterations of traditional symbols. Keeping visual distractions to minimum will enhance performers ability to associate musical symbols with their appropriate sounds.

NOTATION
Note Placement

With respect to note placement, the note value should be reflected in the amount of space it physically takes up in a measure. In common or 4/4 time, a half note should take up one half of the measure; and a quarter note should take up one quarter of the measure etc.

Be conscious of the imaginary bar line at all times. If you are having trouble with note placement lightly draw the imaginary bar line in pencil, and erase later. Note how the imaginary bar line falls in the middle of the measure with equal amounts of time on either side.

Make sure when you're using tablature that the tab aligns with the corresponding melody. Also chord symbols should be over the appropriate beat where the chord sounds.

NOTATION
Stems

Another point of confusion is on which side the stem should be placed. On individual notes from the middle line up, the stem should be on the left side and down.

All notes below the middle line should be to the right and pointing up.

The stem length on individual notes should be one octave. When parts share a staff, up-stem notes above the middle line are shorter than normal, and down-stem notes below the middle line are shorter than normal.

When beaming notes, the furthest note from the middle line dictates the direction of the stem. If the highest note is farther from the middle line than the lowest note, the stems should go down. If the lowest note is

farther from the middle line than the highest note, the stems should go up. If the highest and lowest notes are the same distance from the middle line, the stem direction will depend on how the majority of the stems of the notes other than the highest and lowest would go. In the example below, the highest and lowest notes are both two lines distance from the middle line. Because more of the notes in the measure on the right (not counting the highest and lowest) are down-stems, the group is down-stem. Changing the fifth note (down-stem) B to (up-stem) A, changes the majority to up-stem notes, and so the group becomes up-stem.

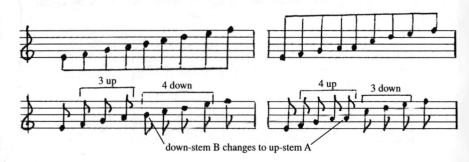

down-stem B changes to up-stem A

28

NOTATION
Stems & Rhythm Notation

The one-octave stem length rule does not apply to notes beyond the first ledger line above or below the staff. All ledger note stems should go to the middle line of the staff.

On notes having up to two flags or beams, do not lengthen the stem to accommodate the additional flag or beam. On notes having three or more flags or beams, lengthen the stem by two notes for each new flag or beam.

Rhythm Notation

Rhythm is commonly notated using slash marks which are thick lines slightly slanted to the right. They extend from the 2nd to the 4th lines of the staff. When indicating 4 beats to the bar, or "time playing", it is not necessary to use stems.

Rhythm section instruments are often given parts indicating chord symbols with specific patterns.

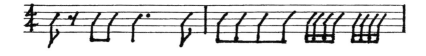

A good general rule, for rhythm parts specifically and contemporary music in general, is to strive for four measures per line, and to start all rehearsal letters and phrases at the beginning of a line whenever possible.

SUMMARY

Hopefully, I've piqued your interest in this important facet of music. Obviously, I've barely scratched the surface of theory, harmony or notation, but merely have highlighted what I feel are the most common areas of misconception.

After all, your music deserves to look as good as it sounds and it is also a great asset to be aware of the inner working of this marvelous art form.

Keep this text in your instrument case, making it easy to get to when questions arise.

Please feel free to email me with any questions, comments or suggestions at: cchapman@berklee.edu

OTHER PRODUCTS BY CHARLES CHAPMAN

Bass Line Basics for Guitar book/CD set (MB98387BCD)

Drop-2 Concept for Guitar book (MB98181)

Finger Gymnastics book/CD set (MB98751BCD)

Making the Changes book/CD set (MB99069BCD)

George Van Eps/Guitar Solos book/CD set (MB94822BCD)

Interviews With The Jazz Greats...and more! book (MB99489)

ABOUT THE AUTHOR

Charles Chapman is a Professor in the Guitar Department at Berklee College of Music where he has taught since 1972. He is a versatile jazz guitarist with extensive performing and recording experience. Charles holds a Bachelors degree from Berklee College and a Masters of Education from Cambridge College. He performed four tunes on the Mel Bay compilation CD "Anthology of Jazz Guitar Solos" and all nine solos on the CD that accompanies the text "Guitar Solos" by George Van Eps (MB94822BCD) and has just released a solo CD titled *Come Sunset*. Charles has published eight texts with Mel Bay Publications and now performs on a regular basis at Guitar Shows and jazz festivals internationally. As a music journalist he has interviewed many of the most prominent guitarists in the field and is a frequent contributor to *Guitar Player, Acoustic Guitar, Fender Frontline, 20th Century Guitar, Mel Bay Guitar Sessions, All About Jazz, Downbeat* and *Just Jazz Guitar* magazines with over 400 published articles and reviews.

Photo by Alistair Mulhearn

Charles has appeared in concert with such luminaries as Martin Taylor, Kenny Burrell, Joe Negri, Jimmy Bruno, Frank Vignola, John Pisano, Ted Greene, Carol Kaye, Jerry Jemmott and Dwane Dolphin.

Charles is an Artist Endorser for *Fender/Guild Corporation* and *Benedetto Guitars*.

EXCELLENCE IN MUSIC